EXECUTIVE ADVICE TO THE YOUNG—

DON'T REPEAT MY MISTAKES!

by

Tom Casey & Gino Piaggio Valdez

Discussion Partners

TELEMACHUS PRESS

Cover designed by Telemachus Press, LLC

Cover art:
Copyright © Dreamstime_47973408_Gloria Rosazza

Published by Telemachus Press, LLC
http://www.telemachuspress.com

Contact the author at:
www.discussionpartners.com

ISBNs:
978-1-942899-89-1 (eBook)
978-1-942899-90-7 (paperback)

Version 2016.05.13

10 9 8 7 6 5 4 3 2 1

Testimonials

My career has been quite a ride resulting in being the Chief Executive of a global Process Improvement advisory firm. Undoubtedly the biggest benefit I had was being mentored by the earliest guru in Total Quality Dr. Joseph Juran who began writing on the topic in the 1940s. One of the lessons I learned from him, was leadership is driven by values and consistency. I believe the recognition of mistakes made in youth, and we all make them, and embedding the lessons learned into a positive leadership style, is the most important result of the book authored by Tom and Gino.

Dr. Joseph Defeo
Chief Executive Officer
Author of *Juran's Quality Essentials for Leaders*
Juran Global Inc.
Boston, MA

Tom Casey and Gino Piaggio's latest book Executive Advice To Young—Don't Repeat My Mistakes!*, is well written and instructive for all readers. Chock full of case studies it provides life and business lessons from a series of successful people who share what they wished they knew when they were younger. Touching and emotional throughout, it shows that in order to succeed in business and life, you need to be true to yourself, your colleagues and your loved ones.*

Michael Dover
Managing Partner Socialstruct Advisory Group
Author of Wikibrands: *Reinventing Your Company In A Customer Driven Marketplace* and the upcoming book-
***Dante's Infinite Monkey's* (working title)**
Toronto, Canada

Wow what a focus for a book! The insights that Tom and Gino embed in the book Executive Advice To Young—Don't Repeat My Mistakes! *on the most regretted decisions is truly provocative. Most baby boomer executives, asked to share mistakes they have made, can talk for hours. And from my own research I know members of younger generations are keen observers, eager to learn. The willingness of these older executives to share painful moments, is a great tutorial for all ages.*

Tammy Erickson (www.tammyericson.com)
Chief Executive Officer Tammy Erickson Associates
Adjunct Professor, Organizational Behaviour London Business School
Four Time Recipient of the Thinkers50 award for Global Business Thought Leadership
Author of a trilogy of books on generations in the workplace including *What's Next Generation X?*
Boston, MA and London, England

My career has had an interesting progression, advanced degree, research oriented advisor, and Chief Executive of a global Political Risk advisory firm. As my interest and experience has been in political leadership and the resultant consequences on societies, ethical motivation is a non-trivial influencer. I have worked with Tom Casey over the last several years. Given all that is going on in the world, I find his and Gino's focus to be timely in that it target's what the executive would change, in the hopes that their mistakes will not be repeated.

Dr. Robert Johnston
Chief Executive Officer
The Eurasia Group
Washington, D.C

I have had an interesting life, model, consultant, athlete, company founder, and parent of two rambunctious boys! This progression has afforded me the opportunity to observe human behavior in extremis, terrific to horrible. I have worked with Tom Casey in various capacities for a decade. I am not surprised, and as he had done for me on several occasions impressed that he would not only have the idea for this book, nor the ability to have the executives forthcoming with what had to be difficult memories. We are never to old to learn...nor share!

David Kruzner
Founder and Partner
Kruzner Karamuru & Associates
Cincinnati, Ohio

When one chooses Accountancy as a profession, as I did decades ago, a realistic conclusion is that this person favors precision vs. abstraction. Yet as one's career advances the human dimensions of motivation, values, fairness, and compassion are the key influencers in the determination of comfort with clients, and colleagues. I have worked with Tom Casey in the past and I applaud he and Gino for asking provocative questions: but more importantly the willingness of the executives to be forthcoming sharing their experiences.

Jorge Medina
President-Proetica, Peruvian Chapter Transparency
International
Retired Managing Partner E&Y Lima Peru
Lima, Peru

As a senior executive with a global company, life can be challenging. Being a father is not without its moments either. Doing the right thing because it is the right thing is a value I want to promote in both capacities. The book authored by Gino and Tom is refreshing as it starts with the premise of misdeed and regret. The transference of lessons learned to the next generation is an intriguing concept and one as a parent and leader should be emulated.

Javier Rehder
Managing Director—Marsh Rehder
Lima, Peru

Table of Contents

EXECUTIVE ADVICE TO THE YOUNG—

DON'T REPEAT MY MISTAKES!

Dedications

Tom Casey
My appreciation to all the Cs in my life, nuclear and extended; to my Peruvian family, who has made me feel most welcome; and of course, to the Renners.

Gino Piaggio Valdez
To my mother and father for their continuous support and affection. To my brothers for their friendship. To Francesca for her love and patience. And to my grandmother Mechita for sharing her life lessons with me.

The Cousins (Catherine, Tricia, & Casey)
We would like to thank our mothers, not only for their personal support, but also for their professional role modeling and mentorship. We are well prepared to contribute and lead in any setting, whether it be a boardroom, classroom, or kitchen table.

Tobey Choate
To my sons Sam and Harrison who have the foresight and tenacity to thrive in the millennial world.

The Sisters (Ada Zane & Zohy Dakota)
We would like to thank our parents, family in both Massachusetts and South Dakota, friends, classmates, and teachers in Vermont.

Introduction—Premise of This Book

THE LAST SEVERAL years have been turbulent. In the US political arena there is a contentious and acrimonious contest for the Presidency. In Peru, concerns about the 2016 election, while at the forefront of many minds, pale with increasing concerns about personal security.

As adults we look at the world around us and should cringe: Pre-adolescent children, whose families aspire to better lives washed up on a Turkish shore, a child purposely left on a beach in Boston and taking months to identify, a steady stream of terrorist attacks, ongoing military actions, corruption without consequences and on it goes!

Watching CNN or the BBC now requires Xanax in advance.

Shame on us! Even more shame on those of us who, through accident of birth, luck, or even hard work, have benefited from what the world has to offer.

As executive men and women, we participate, contribute, and promote good works. The authors take the view that this is no longer sufficient and should be perceived as a threshold obligation.

Moreover we, the authors, take the view that there is a compelling opportunity for executives to make a sustainable contribution by creating learning moments for our children and grandchildren. We can do this by sharing those decisions for which, to this day, we are still ashamed of—or at least a bit embarrassed by.

On a more benign level, reinforcing legacy insights learned from one's parents, and sharing that point of view from the platform of adulthood can create powerful learning moments, as well.

With this as a backdrop, the authors began a process of executive interviews with the following questions: "As a young person did you ever do anything that to this day you regret, despite your age and success? Is there a behavior you would not want your children or grandchildren to repeat?"

The author's premise is that children prefer to hear the realities of mistakes and their lessons learned as opposed to being preached at by adults on an abstract basis of what is 'right or wrong.'

During the creation of this book the authors were struck by four insights:
1. The willingness of the executives to share embarrassing moments,
2. On average, 27 years later, these lapses in judgment remain front of mind,
3. Comfort in sharing with the authors did not translate into comfort communicating their 'failures'; emotions remained intense, and
4. The reinforcement of the adage 'doing the right thing in the first place reduces the number of times one has to apologize.

Tom Casey—Boston, USA
Gino Piaggio Valdez—Lima, Peru

Chapter 1:
I Was Ashamed—Now I Am Again

OUR FIRST INTERVIEW was with a Boston based executive who had an extensive career in the US military as a senior reserve officer in tandem with his commercial role.

The executive was commenting on reactions in the US post-Paris, San Bernardino, and Brussels terror attacks. He was appalled that candidates were debating the wisdom of registration by religious affiliation and the exclusion of Muslim entry into the US. It was a position he found "embarrassing as an American and moreover as a human being."

Interview

September 11th, 2001, changed much for us in the States. We no longer felt safe, and for the most part, we were unclear who the enemy was. In decades past, it was a country vs. a country not a society vs. a religious belief kidnapped by extremists for their own purposes.

I have to say, though, in the aftermath I behaved very badly on one specific occasion for which I am still ashamed.

About a week after 9/11, I boarded a plane from Boston to Dallas. I was upgraded to First Class as the plane was somewhat empty.

Shortly after I boarded another passenger came on who looked of Arabic descent. I gave him a look that, at best, could be described as rage, if not overtly threatening.

Immediately after he took his seat, also in First Class, I took off my belt, rolled it up into a garrote, and covered it with my jacket. Candidly, I don't know what I would have done if he had moved towards the cockpit...likely something stupid.

Fortunately, he did not get out of his seat.

When we landed, I felt awful and guilty.

I waited for him in the terminal and apologized for the look I gave him with the words, "I am sorry, that was inappropriate, and I thought I was better than that."

The man was startled that I took the time to wait, never mind apologize. He was Iranian and had come to the States as a student in the 80s and never went back due to the change in leadership and societal culture.

He did say, "I guess I have to get used to people being suspicious and focusing their anger on me. I am angry, too, for what has been done to <u>us</u>!"

Executive Insights

The word to remember is 'us.' This man felt the same way I did about the terrorist attack.

It is dangerous to blame a society, religion, or philosophy for the actions of a few.

Other than Native Americans, everyone in the US has immigrant origins. The only difference is how many generations exist between our ancestors and us. Ignoring this or forgetting one's heritage is short sighted in the extreme!

Chapter 2:
Saying You're Sorry Isn't Good Enough!

THE NEXT INTERVIEW was with a Los Angeles based real estate executive who, at age 18, entered the US Army during the Viet Nam War.

When asked about his lifelong regret, without hesitation he said, "I contributed to someone committing suicide."

When relating his story, it became obvious that he was clearly anguished over 50 years later.

The story he related was chilling.

Interview

When I began basic training, I joined a group of people who were like me, young, scared, and seeking reassurance. You have to remember there was a war on in Southeast Asia, and we were likely to be sent there (he later served in Viet Nam).

During our basic training, one guy who joined us clearly did not fit in. He was girlish, not strong, and cried all the time. What we should have done was help him, but we did the opposite. We ridiculed him, isolated him, and told him he wouldn't survive in 'Nam.

About three weeks into our training he took his own life.

I could have done something, but I didn't. I was struggling to find my own way then, and when I think of it now it is a weak excuse.

I was pathetic. Even if I wanted to say I'm sorry there was no way that was enough.

Executive Insights

Recognize that some people feel leaving the world is better than coping with their discomforts and/or sadness, particularly when they feel unsupported or might feel it is in their loved one's best interests.

If you don't take this into consideration by trying to help, and something terrible happens, you are indirectly responsible.

Saying that you are sorry when sincere is highly recommended, except in circumstances that are way too late.

There is no excuse for sitting on the sidelines when others are being hurt or harassed. It is the mark of a coward.

Author's Note

The advent of social media has elevated juvenile suicide to epidemic proportions. Juvenile suicide is now the third leading cause of death for 15 to 24 year olds (American Society for Pediatrics).

Depression and bipolar disorders, which are prevalent in children or in situations involving school abuse, are exacerbated by what the authors label as "cloud condemnation." This is using social media as an instrument of abuse while trying to retain distance or even more cowardly, anonymity.

We as adults and young adults are aware that the advantages of social media are very worthwhile. However, we need to be mindful that abuse of this vehicle can be dangerous, if not deadly.

Author's Suggestion

Ask yourself the question: "When reading a negative post about a classmate or acquaintance, how would I feel or react if this was about me?"

Chapter 3:
Billy Got Big!

THE NEXT EXECUTIVE has a son who is a middle school teacher with an outstanding reputation. He has followed in the footsteps of his teaching mentor and always wears a tie to work. When a mural was created by the school's students, as a tribute to his effectiveness, he was one of the few teachers illustrated, distinguishable by his tie.

<u>Interview</u>

Both my son and his wife are teachers. We began discussing the concept of this book with the agreement that he would be interviewed. The first topic we discussed was bullying and its effects on children.

My son said, "Okay, I have to come clean. When I was in second grade I really teased other kids a lot, and one of the kids I teased the most was Billy B.

"I never thought of it as cruel, and bullying is not how I remember it. But I should have realized I was hurting his feelings.

"He did get payback, though, when we got to high school. I hadn't seen him in a while.

"A few days after we started school a friend came to me and said, 'Bill B. is looking for you and he got big!'

"I didn't think anything of it until later. I closed my locker and there stood Billy B. and he was huge! He started beating on me. I don't know if I cried, I just wanted to live until first period."

When I asked, "So what did that teach you…and what do you say to your own kids (who are rather big for their ages) and students?"

His response: "Well, I tell them it is wrong. But I also tell them that eventually teasers and bullies run into a Billy B. and they will pay. I tell my fifth grader's the same story when they lay hands on each other."

Executive Insights

Being a bully is beneath the courage and identity of intelligent individuals. Anyone with a brain should be self aware. The victims of bullies NEVER forget and, like Billy, if they are in a position to hurt you to get even they will.

Using social media as a vehicle to abuse and intimidate is like un-firing a gun…impossible. Those who engage in this exercise are true cowards, and their behavior is beneath contempt. And be advised, despite outward expressions, to the contrary no one will ever trust you.

Chapter 4:
Parents Were Once People Too!

WE WERE SPEAKING to a New York based executive recently about her high school years.

She, let's call her Jeannie, told an interesting story…

Jeannie grew up in Brooklyn and attended a Catholic girls school where the students had a dress code. She had parents who adored her, but they were strict.

On her last day of high school, she and two friends thought it would be great fun to go to a nearby Irish pub named Devlin's to celebrate.

The drinking age in New York was 18. Jeannie's friends were of age, but she was not.

The bartender was used to seeing students from the school celebrating their last day and did not ask for identification.

The ladies were playing pool and having a beer when, lo and behold, one of their teachers, Sister Luisa Teresa, stood before them and said, "Ladies, what are you thinking, you are in a bar in clear sight of our school, embarrassing us, yourselves, and your families.

And I am not sure you are all old enough to drink." She went on to say, "We are leaving now, and if I don't hear from your parents by Monday, you won't graduate." She may have been inclined to add the last part when one of Jeannie's friends asked, "Can we finish our beer?"

The three girls were worried and embarrassed. They decided to meet to discuss what to do. Jeannie's friends had to explain to their parents why that day was a good to day to go to the pub. However, Jeannie had to explain why she was in the pub in the first place.

As often happens when in trouble, you have to decide which parent to tell. Jeannie thought of her father as 'more understanding' and her mother as 'more strict.' She decided, given the circumstances, that she should start with her mother.

Jeannie called her saying "Mom, I am in trouble." She stopped while her mother asked, "Are you hurt? Was anyone else hurt, etc.?" She said, "No I was in Devlin's with two friends." Jeannie was all set with some creative excuses when her mother blurted out, "How did you get caught?" Not the response Jeannie had expected.

It turned out that Jeannie's mother had also celebrated at Devlin's the day she graduated from the same school!

Her mother handled it well. "Okay, I will call the school, but don't tell your father."

Jeannie graduated, and her father learned of her predicament "about five years later."

Executive Insights

It is best to play it smart. You may think your adventures in life are breaking new ground, but that is not likely. Your parents were on the planet first; not much will surprise them.

Chapter 5:
Lying Hurts Everyone!!!!

THE AUTHORS INTERVIEWED a number of executives on the topic of lying. We came away somewhat depressed as everyone seemed to—if not lie—really exaggerate when they were younger. Nobody could remember really good reasons other than to "get out of trouble."

We decided that, among the many examples where honesty was not the best policy, the following shared by a Chicago based media executive provided the most lessons learned.

<u>Interview</u>

A friend and I decided to skip school one day. I attended a Catholic boys elementary school.

We hung out at a coffee shop near the school, which, in hindsight, was not very smart. In fact, it was like we wanted to get caught. And of course we did.

The next day we were summoned to the Mother Superior's office to explain ourselves.

There were no good reasons to skip other than we did not want to go to school that day. However, we did not say that. Instead, we lied.

What embarrasses me to this day is what we said.

We told the Sister that we had, in fact, planned on attending school, but had gone to church beforehand (Lie #1—we did not go to church). We said that after Mass we saw the church custodian who told us, "You don't have to go to school today.

"You can hang out here." (Lie #2—we were not at church, therefore we never saw anyone, and certainly did not get permission to stay there.)

When asked how we then ended up at the coffee shop, we said, "The Custodian told us he was going home and we were going to have to leave." (Lie #3—obviously)

The Mother Superior clearly did not believe us. However, her response, the church's response, and the response of others was a surprise. We were not punished, and the custodian just disappeared!

Be mindful that at the time there was much controversy regarding child abuse by priests.

I can't tell you how many times in the 30 years since then I thought about how stupid and cruel this was for us to do.

When asked, "Did you ever tell the truth or find out what happened to that guy?" No, I never told the truth. But after college, I tracked down the custodian to apologize.

He was much more gracious than I could have been, although he made clear that the lie had ruined his life.

"Kid, they never believed you, but they did not want the controversy, and they took very good care of me." They had relocated him to another Parish. "Though, to this day, I am not trusted. I am never alone around children."

"I would like to say you did me a favor, but to do that I would have to forgive what you did. And I don't."

His parting words were "Liars never are forgiven and always mistrusted. I hope you are smarter now than you were then."

<u>Executive Insights</u>

Telling a lie is guaranteed to make you lose sleep if you are a good person. And if you are not losing sleep get therapy!

If you tell a lie, don't involve innocent people. It is cruel and can cause unspeakable pain.

If you do hurt someone, do the right thing no matter how long it takes to apologize. It may result in forgiveness, at the least, it will make you feel a little more like you belong in the human race.

Chapter 6:
Remember The Alamo

THE AUTHORS HAVE some friends who visited San Antonio on a business trip. During a break they decided to see the local sights such as The River Walk, and of course, the Alamo.

San Antonio can be very hot in September and such was the case that day.

There were a number of tourists waiting to gain entry including a mother with her child, Jennifer.

Interview

Jennifer was hot, cranky, and uncooperative as her mother beseeched her to "stay in the shade." Jennifer's reaction, however, was to say, "No, I don't have to."

For those of you who have visited the Alamo, you know the security officers dress like olden Texas Rangers complete with boots, six shooter belts, and of course the big Stetson.

The mother, in frustration, said within Jennifer's hearing, "Officer, can you help me get my daughter to behave?"

Jen was paying close attention as the officer tipped his hat, said "yes ma'am," hoisted his belt, and began ambling towards our little princess.

Jennifer broke the land speed record racing to her mother saying, "I'm sorry, Mommy."

Executive Insights

Obey your mother when she is trying to be helpful. Remember parents DO usually know best and have for the moment more influence than their children.

Chapter 7:
Stealing is Wrong &
Payback Can be Expensive!

THE AUTHORS GOT a good laugh after talking to this Atlanta based consulting executive who told the following story about stealing a record when he was 12.

Interview

I was in a store with my best friend. We were both into music, and while we were looking at records I saw him stick one underneath his jacket.

I asked him, "What are you doing?" His response was, "You should get one too, we won't get caught."

To my regret, I did take one. I did not get caught. And what is worse, I had the money and could have paid for the record.

I wish I could say I felt bad, I didn't. Or smart, I didn't. I really did not feel anything at all. That came later...

"I can even remember the record, 'Locomotion' by Little Eva. When Grand Funk Railroad covered the song later, every time I heard it, I cringed."

It is easy to say "I will never steal again," and even if you don't, it does not absolve having done it in the first place.

I have to admit, in the odd moment as I got older, I did think about what I did, no excuses, just facts. I recognized that, at that moment, I was weak and stupid.

Fast-forward 30 years when I met the former CEO of the store from which I stole. He was a new client and had become extremely successful since that time.

I decided, better late then never, and told the client about having stolen from his store.

He just stared at me and did not say a word.

The next day he presented me with a bill for $795.19, which was the present day value of the 45 Record.

He asked that I make the check out to a charity he had designated.

I gladly wrote the check!

Executive Insights

Stealing is wrong. There is no circumstance that makes it right.

If you do steal and have a conscience you will never forgive yourself.

No matter how long it takes, make restitution. It won't erase the wrong, but it is a start.

Chapter 8:
In Praise of the Youngest
or Count Yourself Lucky!

OVER THE HOLIDAYS, Tom enjoyed a long overdue dinner with family members. He had just returned from a cruise. During the dinner, however, he realized this was not his 'first' cruise, as he had erroneously been communicating.

In point of fact, he had been on a family cruise 50 years earlier. He had forgotten. This was not an issue of repressed memory or trauma. Well, maybe a little trauma!

The catalyst for recollection was the dinner discussion regarding family sequence, oldest child, middle child, and youngest child.

Two of us at the table were the 'oldest' and our spouses 'middle.' So, we thought it only fair to be hypercritical of the benefits derived from being the youngest.

What does this have to do with a cruise 50 years ago?

Interview

During the cruise we had a respite in a Canadian resort where the young staff members referred to the guests as 'the newlywed, the nearly dead, and the overfed.'

Being invaded by an American Irish family of seven children, with a particularly gregarious and loud father, and a tolerant mother, might be disruptive.

And it was for the guests. But the wait staff and others went out of their way to be assigned to us because we were fun.

Granted, based on observation, their definition of 'fun' might have been described as 'having a pulse.'

But, back to the topic, the benefits accrued by being the youngest.

During the stay, our four-year-old sister thought it would be a brilliant idea to pretend to disappear. This prompted a search of the hotel, the waterline, etc. by family members, hotel staff, etc.

We eventually found our princess hiding under the bed, all the while thinking this attention was just fantastic!

What struck me at the time, beyond universal relief, was the lack of recrimination by our parents. Notwithstanding some minor 'don't you ever' sentiments, I thought—if it had not been her—the associated punishment would have bordered on corporal!

Years later, as I was entering the military, I asked my father who was the youngest in his family—why the difference?

His response was, 'I can speak from experience. The younger you are in most families, the more tolerant are the parents.' My father went on to say 'and thus it is written. I did not ask 'where.'

Of course, in his family he was the youngest. The oldest in his family once admonished her daughter, 'You were born into the #1 slot in the family. Your siblings will spend the rest of their lives trying to get there.'

I have always appreciated the wisdom of my aunt and cousin.

In closing, Tom reverted back to his youngest sister. "She was always quiet to the point we had to make sure she was not left behind in restaurants, hotels etc., given the numerical disadvantage she suffered having six older siblings."

"We were the Lowell, MA, version of 'Home Alone.'"

At given times, each of my brothers and sisters and I were assigned the task of 'not forgetting your sister' by our parents.

On one occasion at a concert, she did manage to slip away. She was later found sitting in the dressing room of the Four Seasons (Jersey Boys), in Frankie Valli's lap explaining how he should comb his hair.

As one of my brothers ventured: " 'Often forgotten…but never lost.'

Executive Insights

Timing IS everything particularly the birthing sequence.

For those of you who are the oldest, as is the case of both authors, we feel your pain!

For the middle child, we concur that you are often overlooked. However, suck it up. If you are looking for adoration download Paul Simon's *Slip Sliding Away!* Often you also are pardoned as well!

For those of you who are the youngest, don't venture too far out on the ice when it is sunny! You also can be surprised by timing! Cute isn't everything!

Chapter 9:
Women Deserve the Same Consideration as Men

THE AUTHORS INTERVIEWED a Washington based executive about his most embarrassing moment when he was younger. He indicated that it was when he tried to be "a big man with my male classmates...I became a little boy with my female classmates."

Interview

When I was younger, I was the teacher's pet. I was always well behaved and the smartest in the class.

One day the teacher had to leave the room and said, "Ray you're in charge until I get back." Unfortunately, she was gone way too long and returned to total chaos. She was less than thrilled.

The teacher asked me to explain myself and I blamed it all on one girl, Brenda. I said she started teasing the boys about being "geeks and weirdos."

You have to remember, back in primary school girls 'weren't really people.' When the executive was asked why he picked Brenda, he replied, "She was so different and quiet I did not think the girls would defend her." They didn't!

After class Brenda came up to me and said, "I thought better of you, Ray."

When we asked, "How did you feel after this incident?" Ray replied, "Like I had no guts. She never spoke to me during the six years we were in school together after that."

She did me a favor though. I never disrespected a girl or woman again. This has helped me out with my wife, two daughters, the women I have worked for and with, and granddaughters

When the authors asked, "What happened to Brenda?" Ray just chuckled. "She is as beautiful as any model, and doing well as a wealthy technology entrepreneur in North Carolina."

<u>Executive Insights</u>

Scapegoating is cowardly no matter what the reason.

Thinking a girl can be offered up to avoid embarrassing your male friends has multiple outcomes…none of them good! Boy/girl awkwardness is expected and is also a rite of passage. However, it is inexcusable when hurtful, particularly if your objective is self-importance.

Chapter 10:
The Benefits of Growing Up in a Multi-Generational Setting

IN HER TRILOGY of books on the generations, *What's Next Generation X?*, Tammy Erickson compellingly asserts that the younger generations, Generation X and the millennial generation, rely heavily on the advice given to them by their parents, and their Boomer supervisors.

The authors, cognizant of their own heritage, postulated that in the US these age cohorts would be as likely to listen to "external Boomers" such as professors or supervisors, as they likely leave home at 18. This conclusion is highlighted in Tammy's works.

We were curious, given the multi-generational nature of cohabitation in South America, if this balance between parents and others would be preserved in Peru as a representative society.

The profile of those interviewed in this blind study was as follows:
>Millennial cohort
>University graduate (graduate degree possible)
>Employed in a professional capacity or, in US parlance, a 'white collar' role
>Living with parents or extended family

The two questions posed were straightforward:
1. What good advice were you given?
2. Did you follow this advice?

Interviews

Administrator for a logistics company

1. What good advice were you given?

"My mom told me, before I entered university, to investigate the careers that interested me before choosing one. 'Be 100 percent sure that you want to study what you choose,' she said. Because of her I know besides liking a career, you have to be sure that it will provide you vast work opportunities in the future."

2. Did you follow her advice?

"Of course I did. I was not sure what was best for me: studying psychology or administration. Finally, I chose administration because it's a career that offers more job opportunities than psychology. As an administrator I can work in different types of companies in diverse areas or create my own business. I started working in the financial department of a bank, then I got a job as a saleswoman in a telephone company, and now I work in the marketing department of a logistics operator."

Lawyer for an Insurance Company

1. What good advice were you given?

"Family and friends have always told me to persevere. I think that's pretty good advice. It means to never give up no matter what. Follow your dreams and don't complain if you don't achieve your goals. Just keep on trying."

2. Have you followed their advice?

"Always. I wouldn't be where I am now if I hadn't. Through perseverance I was able to become the Peruvian championship in Tae Kwon Do, and I was able to enter the Peruvian sailing team and win the international championship with my teammates. Because of perseverance, I finished school, entered university, obtained a master's degree, and finally got the job I always dreamed about. There were many setbacks on the way, but they didn't stop me."

<u>Industrial Engineer</u>

1. What good advice have you been given?

"My grandfather told me to set smart goals. At first I thought it meant quitting your dreams, but it really means detecting your abilities, developing them, setting goals based on those abilities, and, wherever you can chasing those dreams. It was good advice because goals are also dreams, but possible dreams. Chasing the impossible will frustrate you, but you can try from time to time if you have the means, money and time, you can obtain the means by achieving your goals."

2. Have you followed his advice?

"Of course. I was really good at numbers, so I decided to study something in that area. At first I thought of physics, that's how much I love numbers. But then I realized that it would be difficult to make a living in Peru as a physicist. I eventually decided to study industrial engineering. I have a good job, which I enjoy. However, in my spare time I teach mathematics, which I enjoy even more."

Entrepreneur

1. What good advice have you been given?

"My father always told me: Fight for what you want to do. To fight is not just to persevere. Fight means to stand up for your goals, face anyone who gets in your way. You have to strive, play fair, and be willing to make a few enemies. Maybe a lot of people want what you want, so you have to want it more, and you have to be ready to hurt feelings. We live in a competitive world. Scruples are good, but they cannot be an advantage for others."

2. Have you followed his advice?

"I have, and thanks to it I am a renowned bullfighter in Peru. I worked on TV for a couple of months and now I am a partner in two companies. And the best is that I have not made enemies, because nowadays, everyone knows that the competition is huge. We live on a globalized planet, so we often have to compete against people from the other side of the world. But you also have to see the bright side of this: Opportunities are endless."

Marine Biologist

1. What good advice have you been given?

"Never follow advice. That's the best advice I've ever been given. But I don't follow it because it's advice. I think all advice is good, especially that which comes from older people because they have more experience. But you have to be careful about the advice you follow because we are all different. The situations we face are unique. Maybe advice 'x' worked for your brother, but it won't work for you. For example, my father always suggested to me and my brother to get a job in a bank because, according to him, that's where the money is. I'm sure all parents want their kids to have money, they don't want them to be poor, but working in a bank is not the only way to prevent poverty. I would have been miserable working in a bank, and I've never needed a lot of money to be happy. However, my brother loves cars and big cigars. I'm joking. He always wanted a big family: Lots of kids, a nice wife, and a couple of dogs. For lots of kids you need lots of money, so he became a lawyer, and a really good one. I, on the other hand, became a marine biologist. I've always loved diving, so I was determined to work the rest of my life near the sea. Everybody thought I would end up on the streets, even I thought that was a possibility. But there was no other way for me. The funny thing is that I've been working as a marine biologist for five years now, and I can afford lots of kids, a nice wife, and a couple of dogs."

Psychologist

1. What good advice have you been given?

"I've been given a lot of advice, but my favorite is: To bad weather, good face. My mother gave it to me. One must always try to be positive no matter how bad the situation. The fury of positivity is amazing. It will help you mentally, physically, professionally and socially."

2. Have you followed that advice?

"Always, and I repeat it to my patients all the time. Some people confuse having their feet on the ground with negativity, and they don't face their problems. They just give up. Others make their problems even worse, and they drown in them. Thanks to positivity I have always found a way out. Positive energy attracts positive things. It attracts success and keeps failure away. It attracts solutions. We will always have problems. The secret to overcoming them is to believe deeply that we can overcome them. If we are not 100 percent convinced, then it will be harder."

Journalist

1. What good advice have you been given?

"A high school teacher once said to me: Be always one step ahead of possible scenarios. That advice has stayed with me ever since. To me it means to take time before making a decision, evaluate the pros and cons of an action, and don't act impulsively."

2. Have you followed that advice?

Not always. Sometimes I act impulsively. For example, when I interview people I always have a draft of questions. However, sometimes I get out of line and start improvising. You can obtain a great interview by acting spontaneously. However, if I go blank, I can refer to the draft questions. Therefore, I don't really consider it acting impulsively because I have the draft, which is my backup plan. I do act impulsively in confrontations with colleagues because of the heat of the moment. But I'm working on that. It is essential to maintain a good working environment. I think that if I keep messing with the working environment at my job, a possible scenario for me could be the street."

Executive Insights

The interviews suggest that most of the advice that Peruvians follow comes from their families. In Peru, family greatly influences children as it is a multi-generational society. Although this is changing, most likely Peruvians will continue to live with their parents and family until they marry.

The foundation of Peruvian society is family, and these relationships are influential and of critical importance.

In the US, children leave home at approximately 18 years old. Picture a late twenty-something coming home from work where parents want to talk about the day or want to discuss why the young person was partying so hard over the weekend.

The multi-generational family is changing in Peru for some. For example, several of those interviewed were living in apartments with friends or were in the process of doing so.

However, for many young Peruvians including one of the co-authors, it is currently the norm.

To the question of why the tradition is being challenged. It is clear that influence sometimes turns into control, and, in Peru, this often happens when young adults return to the house of their parents after living abroad. That being said, we can conclude that Peruvians and American Millennials are similar in our respect for parents and elders. It is not accidental or coincidental that close to ALL of those interviewed identified the source of their advice as family members.

For Peruvians, remaining in the parental home until one is married has some advantages. For example, discretion as to how to spend the money one earns. There is no need to spend money on rent or on a maid. Generally, in Peru, upper class and middle class people have maids in their houses. They tend the beds, clean the house, wash the clothes, buy the groceries, cook, serve the table and clean the dishes. This is obviously comfortable, and if one is living with his or her parents, it is free. When we mention this to our US friends they want to relocate!

However, there are also disadvantages. Despite being of age, you are still living in a house that's not yours, so you have to follow the owners' rules, usually your parents. Also, you don't have the privacy that you would have if you lived away from home, and this can cause problems with relationships. This could be why Peruvians marry younger!

However, our brief study did answer the question about where one gets advice and the answer is the family. In addition, we asked, Do you follow it? The answer was absolutely. We also asked, Is the family more influential than peers and bosses? The answer was yes. This a fundamental difference within the Peruvian versus US young adult age groups. In general, we can state that a multi-generational residence promotes more interaction, and therefore opportunity, for advice as opposed to those who rely not only on their parents but others such as bosses, colleagues, or friends.

Chapter 11:
Lessons My Mother
Taught Me...Pass It On!

TOM HAS TWO cousins who are both accomplished professionals in the healthcare sector. Between them they have three daughters and four granddaughters.

He noticed, during various interactions with the family, his two cousins promoted learning moments through targeted instructions.

Their three daughters, Catherine, Tricia, and Casey have continued this tradition with their children. The author's speculation is that these sayings are likely to be passed on by the progeny of both his cousins.

He asked the daughters if they could share the lessons learned through these sayings that would apply to girls and younger women.

Below is a sample of the shared parental wisdom.

Nothing good happens after midnight.

No matter what, always wear a slip.

You should date someone for a full year before marriage because you will see how they cope with stress during each of the four seasons.

What you can't figure out, NASA, brain surgery etc., you can learn on the job.

Never criticize your children in public. If they can't depend on you to be their truest supporter, who can they depend on?

If you always have a book with you, you'll never be annoyed when someone is late.

Never let anyone know you can type.

If you are dealing with a difficult person at work, sit next to them at meetings. It is easier to fight with someone across the table, but more difficult if they are right next to you.

You only have one reputation. Once lost it is never returned.

Never acknowledge you can or are willing to do all the grunt work.

Knowing the details is management doing the details means you are understaffed.

Chapter 12:
I Don't Want To Be Arrested!

THE AUTHORS ASKED a Dallas based executive, "Did you ever give a piece of advice that had unintended consequences?" His response was "Oh yeah!"

Interview

A while ago I was leaving a movie with my two grandsons, 12 and 9. Of course, on the way into the film you buy everything in sight, popcorn, candy for emergency purposes, and of course a 'big gulp' soda.

On the way out the 9-year-old refilled his cup. I said to him, "You're not supposed to do that. We have to pay." He felt a little bad, and I told him not to worry about it. He kept saying "I didn't know."

In the car he continued to apologize thinking I was upset.

To reassure him I told both boys about how I once was embarrassed for doing the same thing. I was in the M&M store in Times Square and I thought these big vats of candy were samples. Of course, I just ate and ate. I then noticed that people were loading bags and going to the check out. I realized my mistake and went to the counter with a bag and told them, "I think I owe you double."

The boys were laughing, of course, stupid grandfather!

A couple of weeks later my son called me and said, "You're never going to believe what your grandson did." Of course my imagination ran wild.

He was at the movies, and as he was leaving his friends started filling their big cups. He told them that they were supposed to pay for them. At that point their ride—aka the mother of one of the boys—arrived telling them to hurry because they would be late.

My grandson told her that they had to pay for the sodas. Apparently she didn't hear him. He then asked if she would call his mother to come get him. 'I don't want to be arrested.' That she heard!

She then said "Huh"… and he said "We have to pay for these sodas." Meanwhile Dillinger and Capone were slurping away.

The mother did the right thing and said "Thank you, of course we have to pay."

Executive Insights

Paying when you should is the best approach—no matter how much or how distracted you are at the time.

Adults telling children about embarrassing moments is very helpful because you are admitting being human and they don't feel as bad.

Young or old, watch your sugar intake!

Chapter 13:
Fatherly Advice—The Three
Pillars of Success

TOBEY CHOATE IS a successful executive advisor. He is acutely aware that, his millennial sons must listen closely to what he says and understand what he believes.

His older son is just beginning his career in financial services, while his second son is a student at Harvard.

When the authors explained the intent of this book, he suggested and we agreed that the treatise he was in the process of preparing for his sons, which embodied his parental advice, would be an appropriate chapter for this book.

Interview

My two sons have emerged from successful college experiences and one is now in the workforce. I felt challenged to give them sage advice beyond 'get a job.' In retrospect, I realized this advice would be totally inadequate in terms of context and specificity.

This is what I didn't say, but wish I had, and now I am saying it to my sons.

Now that you are graduating college you feel like you are prepared to take on the world and rocket to success. Congratulations, but this is not true. However you define it, success in life is built on three pillars. Your early years, high school, and college accomplishments have provided the confidence and basic skills to now build a foundation, which you can use to have a successful life.

There are no guarantees for success or happiness; but my belief is that there are three fundamental 'pillars.' If you embed these into your personal outlook, your chances of success and happiness are increased.

<u>The Three Pillars</u>

The pillars are a healthy lifestyle, robust relationships and financial common sense. Here are my suggestions:

> <u>Healthy Lifestyle</u>
> Eat right in content and portions—CANCEL THE PIZZA ORDER IN FAVOR OF A SALAD! Exercise routinely—A SEDENTARY LIFESTYLE IS THE CIGARETTE OF YOUR GENERATION—JUST MOVE.
>
> Expand your mind with new and different experiences and thoughts—READ BOOKS AND CULTIVATE FRIENDS NOT LIKE YOU.
>
> <u>Robust Relationships</u>
> Build networks from networks—EVERY SCHOOL, JOB AND ORGANIZATION YOU JOIN IS A READY-MADE NETWORK FOR YOU TO LEVERAGE. SHARED EXPERIENCES ARE A POWERFUL BOND.

Help others without question or reward—A SIMPLE ACT OF KINDNESS GOES A LONG WAY; JUST PICKING UP THE PHONE AND SAYING "HOW'S IT GOING?" MAKES A DIFFERENCE

Do not be afraid to ask—FRIENDS LIKE TO HELP FRIENDS; IT MAKES THEM FEEL GOOD TO HELP. SO JUST ASK.

Financial Commonsense

Live within your means and paycheck—PAY Off YOUR DEBTS AND LIVE ON CASH AND VENMO.

Believe in the power of compounding by saving early and often—MAX YOUR 401K, FLEXIBLIE AND HEALTH SAVINGS ACCOUNTS AS IF THEY WERE UNAVOIDABLE TAXES AND LET THEM GROW; FINANCIAL SECURITY IS A MIDDLE-DISTANCE RACE, NOT A SPRINT.

Prune your financial commitments—GO THROUGH A REGULAR COST CUTTNG EXERCISE, ESPECIALLY THOSE AUTOMATICALLY DEDUCTED SMALL MONTHLY FEES THAT ADD UP TO A BIG ANNUAL HEADACHE.

Chapter 14:
How Do Liberals React
When They Learn They Are Racist??

IT HAS BEEN a difficult period for tolerance in the world. The US political landscape clearly is anti-immigration to the point of building walls to "keep them out." Europe the influx of migrants is challenging many societal norms and institutions.

In the US Police relations are strained with comedians venturing, "The only way to avoid being shot is (a) don't wear a hoodie, (b) don't be big and (c) don't be Black." Somehow, we think this is funny!

It is easy to be sardonic when we hear the words "Black lives matter" and respond "All lives matter." Yet focusing on the US reality is much different.

Years ago there was a TV series, 'L.A. Law,' which some of you may remember. If not, there is always Hulu.

In one episode, to compel a judge to recuse himself from the trial of a Black defendant, the lawyers presented him with statistical evidence that his decisions and sentencing outcomes were blatantly racist.

When presented with such evidence, one would expect the character (or a real-life person who feels they are open minded) to be defensive.

In the episode, the judge did the right thing, he recused himself. He was self-aware enough to know he was not self-aware.

Intolerance is ugly. As this chapter is being written, Pope Francis is characterizing the desire to build walls as "Un-Christian." Unfortunately his point of view is not endorsed by many.

The authors started with the premise that we are all intolerant in some way. This is not part of our DNA; it is learned behavior. The question before us was twofold: (a) How did you know that your self-image was delusional and (b) What do you do when you are faced with your subconscious intolerance?

We were fortunate to find an executive who was willing to share his experiences. What is of particular interest in this interview is that this executive held Congressional office in the past and was known as an advocate for tolerance on multiple issues.

Interview

During my formative years I was privileged. Consequently my personal philosophy and points of view about race relations, immigration, and other issues were based on reading and discussions, not experience.

I always thought of myself as tolerant regarding people who were different, whether it is race, political orientation, sexual preference, etc.

Unfortunately I was wrong…

I was giving a speech out of state and got lost on the way back to the airport.

This was in the days before iPhones, so lost meant lost. I had someone with me who was driving the rental car.

We wandered into a not-so-nice neighborhood and stopped to get our bearings. I noticed three young men of color not far away who were clearly aware of our presence. We were scared! They started walking toward us, and in an attempt to drive away we crashed the car.

They kept coming. They were actually running. When they got to us they said, "Are you guys okay?" "Do you need some help?" They could not have been nicer…they got us to the airport, arranged for the rental car company to come…" They were great."

Flying back home, I could not help thinking about how scared I was and why. Clearly it was the neighborhood, the circumstances, and more importantly that the three young men were Black.

I asked myself the question "Even in a rough neighborhood, if they had been white, dressed in khaki's wearing IZOD shirts, would I have reacted the same way?"

Clearly not…

When I look back on that event, I realized that even with a narrow definition of the word, I am really a racist. It shook my self-image and I try to be mindful that is 'who I am, not who I thought I was.'

"The question before me at that time was: How could I channel this awareness minimizing the damage it could cause? Maybe I could even use the awareness to do some good."

What got my attention though was when I relayed what happened to others, their response was disheartening as they commented, "I would have been scared, too." Also "you got lucky."

Executive Insights

We are all intolerant of some things or many things, either consciously or subconsciously, when we are confronted with our true beliefs or tendencies, we can behave in one of two ways: ignore it, or attempt to channel it in appropriate ways.

Self-awareness is an asset, self-respect an aspiration, and self-direction in positive ways is an obligation, even when it confronts who you really are as a person.

Chapter 15:
You Own Your Choices!

IT IS VERY hard to find a graceful way to end a book that blends insights of executives derived from lapses in judgment, parental wisdom passed down, and comparison of US and South American young adulthood.

During our writing, the authors could not help but be mindful of others who have given public advice.

The Ten Commandments are repeatedly broken, the Torah misinterpreted, and unspeakable acts of cruelty are committed in the name of Mohammed, who was at his core was a pacifist.

We are 16 years into a century that began with terrorism, corruption without consequences, and political paralysis.

There is no institutional or societal reason to feel optimistic about imminent change.

The authors were inspired by executives who were willing to be forthcoming with very difficult incidents, who could have easily refused.

Alternatively, they embraced the idea of avoiding the metaphor "We have met the enemy and they are us" in favor of "If I can share via this vehicle it may be helpful in some small way."

However, the authors feel that to do justice to what we learned, and leapfrog over the appropriate advice of 'don't steal, don't bully etc.,' we must synthesize what we derived from our interactions.

The advice of the executives we interviewed is straightforward, self-evident and should be followed.

However, as we augment their suggestions, transitioning them to principles, we offer the following:

Think of the consequences—it is very difficult to project how one will feel, who may be hurt, or other implications of lapsed judgment, although not impossible. There should at least be an attempt to "future forward" in the hopes that mistakes can be avoided based upon outcomes.

Social Media Responsibility—Facebook and other vehicles are both an asset and a liability. If we focus on the liability when the capability is used to intimidate or punish, one should be mature enough to know this is cowardly and wrong. Before you start typing away, stop and think "What if what I am writing was being written about me?"

Respect for The Unfamiliar—respect for those we know and like is not a challenge. Respect for those who are different and who espouse a point of view you disagree with is more difficult. Yet no matter where we turn, or what we turn on, there is ambiguity. Overreactions complicate an already difficult situation. You don't have to agree; but you should at least respect.

<u>Exercising Judgment</u>—no one is born with a DNA that compels bad decisions. How an individual behaves is the objective manifestation of freedom of choice. The reason inappropriate judgment is exercised is based upon expediency. Stepping away from doing what is easy is hard...but necessary.

<u>Family Matters</u>—the dynamics of any family are complex regardless of age or circumstance. The fact that the younger generation has demonstrated the wisdom to listen to their elders is a great step and one to be applauded, even when there is family tension.

There are many examples of bad behavior or imperfect judgment in this book. There is also redemption; not because those interviewed feel less bad about their transgressions, but their willingness to share may create an opportunity for others to avoid making the same mistakes.

This book will never rival *War and Peace*, will never be made into a movie, nor will it ever make a reputable best seller list. Our intent as a son, brother, husband, father, and grandparent is to offer up the certainty that as a child or a young adult, you DO have choices...based on the insights derived from those who have shared their bad decisions. Making the right choice is enthusiastically recommended.

About the Contributors

Edward T. "Tobey" Choate—is the Founder and Managing Partner of Choate and Associates, an advisory firm focused on start-up and family owned businesses. He was a contributor to one of Tom Casey's best sellers *Executive Transitions-Plotting The Opportunity!* Tobey can be reached at <u>Choate@choateassociates.com</u>

Catherine Halloran, Tricia Jorden, and Casey Osborne are the daughters of two sisters. In addition to motherhood, each balanced the demands of a distinguished professional career in the healthcare sector. Following in their mothers' footsteps, these cousins have enjoyed distinguished dual careers in marketing and parenting.

Ada Zane (14 years old) and Zohy Dakota Renner (12 years old) are Vermont based elementary school students. They are voracious readers; this proficiency was essential for insuring the narratives in this book could be appreciated by the younger reader. They can be reached through their agent beginning in 2020!

All involved with this book would like to thank Samantha "Sam" Fleury an 11-year-old student in Durham, NH, and Lynn Casey, a teacher in Crystal Lake, Illinois, for their inspiration for this book...

Other Books

Inflection Points—Risk Readiness and Fearless Failure!
Tom Casey and Sean Casey; with Ariana Pazos Aramburú

Talent Readiness—The Future is Now
Tom Casey with Tim Donahue and Eric Seubert

Executive Transitions—Plotting the Opportunity
Tom Casey and Karen Warlin
with Tobey Choate and Sean Casey

CPSIA information can be obtained
at www.ICGtesting.com
Printed in the USA
LVOW12s1424190816
500599LV00001B/1/P